THROUGH THE FIRE

A Devotional Journal to Get You Through The
Trials of Life

Sanura X Dean

Life Chronicles Publishing
Give your life a voice!

www.mylifechronicles.org

Life Chronicles Publishing

ISBN-13:978-0998911458

ISBN- 10: 0998911453

Cover Design: Life Chronicles

Editor: Sahsha Campbell-Garbutt

Dedication:

I dedicate this book to my four beautiful, loving, and intelligent children. Eldridge, Carlos, Jaela, and Danielle. Words cannot express how grateful I am to be the mother of such amazing children. You have loved me, and been a support to me, even when I did not see it myself. I want to personally thank you for being so supportive and loving through the sacrifice of being ministry kids. Thank you for being so tender, generous and caring when I needed it most. There is nothing in the world that you cannot do when you focus in on who and what you are. You are my children, but most importantly, you are the KING'S KIDS. Always keep that in your heart, mind, and spirit. Thank you for all the special times that we have shared together thus far. You make me want to be the best person I can be in every area of my life. I love you more than you know. Never forget, when all else fails...look to Jesus.

Contents

Acknowledgements

It would be wrong of me to write this book and not acknowledge those that have helped me to grow into the woman of God that I am today. I would like to give a heartfelt thank you to everyone that has touched my heart and life. I can't possibly mention everyone's name but if you know me, know that you have been a blessing to me and I thank you.

To my mother, Lillian Mussa: I want to thank you for loving me and nurturing me. I learned many things from you; I am most thankful for how you taught me to be a giver through your example. I love you to the moon and back!

To my Bishop, Zachary K. Bruce Sr: I want to thank you from the bottom of my heart for how you have helped me and my family grow. I have never witnessed a Senior Pastor as genuine as you. Your heart is one of gold, and anyone that has the privilege to sit under you in ministry would know you are a blessing.

To the entire Dean family: Thank you all so much for welcoming me into your family and keeping me. I love you all individually. Each one of you has touched my life in a different way, and I am grateful for the connection. You have taught me what it means to be family.

WITF: My prayer partners and prayer warriors...you know how we get down. Thank you, and I love you so much.

Pastor Sheila: What can I say? Well, a lot actually. Let me just say that there is not space enough here to express how grateful to God I am that He brought you into my life. You hold so many hats in my life. I love you to the moon and back #Bestie #Family #RideorDie

To Dorthey-Inez (AKA DI): Thank you for never giving up on me and always pushing me towards my dreams. Thank you for teaching me to have the confidence to show up and shine and for having my back when I didn't think it was possible.

Prophetess Jessica: Thank you for all your love and support. I thank God for the unexpected bond that we have. Love you much. #mysisterskeeper #twins #absoluetlynot

#officesupplygroupies #NotTodaySatan #AbsouuetlyNot

To My Freedom Church of Seattle Family: Thank you for all
the love and support over the years.

Preface

Dear Sister,

Thank you so much for choosing THROUGH THE FIRE to help you through your process to wholeness and victory from the challenges of life. Let me tell you right now that this book was written while I was going through my process from brokenness to wholeness. During my time of devotion, the Lord inspired me to write a word of truth and open up about what he was saying to me that led me to victory. It was imperative for me to listen so that I would be able to help someone through their fiery trial. During this time of devotion, I was going through one of the hardest times in my life as a woman of God. I thought that when I became a Christian, my life would become untouchable. Sure, I have gone through some trials, but I never thought one of the most valued things that I had in my life would be touched in the way that it was. I never thought in a million years that my vow to stay "till death do us part" would be broken by divorce and that God would use such an experience of brokenness to build me up and fortify me with a greater anointing to do his work. I pray that God touches you through this book the way that he touched me as I was going through the process of healing. Allow God to be God in your life. Trust me; I am a living witness that you can come out like pure GOLD!

In the midst of my journey, my aunt invited me to do a week-long challenge to love myself. It was interesting what God spoke to my heart as I prayed about the different ways I could start this journey. I want to share with you what he said, and I pray that you will take the time to receive this message from the Lord as you read each devotion. He said: "Sanura (insert your name here) do you love yourself enough to surrender to the process of your journey? Do you love yourself enough to surrender to all the Master has to do to mold you through this time of transition? Are you willing to go through the hurt and pain of rejection and the uncertainty? Are you able to love yourself enough to understand that there is something greater in store for you regardless of how you feel?" Isn't that amazing? I was in total awe of God.

Can you understand that God loves you enough to trust you with this test because He knows that you will use it to glorify him? There is purpose in your pain, so hold on to the promise that God will deliver you. It starts with surrender...

I encourage you to embrace the beauty of the present process. You have God on your side, and He is ready to restore you one step at a time. Open yourself up to him as you read, reflect, and journal. I promise that you will never be the same. The thing that I love about our God is that He always restores you beyond what you were before. He is so faithful. Thank you again for choosing this book. I am praying for you.

Love,

Sanura

Chapter One

Constant Gratitude

THE VOICE OF TRUTH:

*IN EVERYTHING GIVE THANKS FOR THIS IS THE WILL OF GOD
IN CHRIST CONCERNING YOU. (1 THESSALONIANS 5:18 NIV)*

As I sit here writing, my marriage is facing divorce. I have no job, and I don't know where the money to pay my bills is going to come. On top of that, my mode of transportation has broken down. It would seem that I don't have much to be thankful for but on the contrary, the Word of God is faithful and will bring me to victory.

I don't know what situation you are facing right now, but God is faithful and will bring you to victory as well.

In everything give thanks. Even when life seems to have fallen apart, we have the opportunity to give thanks for the truth that as believers we serve a loving and all-powerful

1

God. We can offer thanks according to Genesis 22:14 (NIV), that we can count on our God, Jehovah-Jireh (which means "the Lord will provide"). Even when we get ourselves into unfortunate situations, our God is so faithful that he will bless us with his mercy, grace, and compassion.

You see, I wish I could tell you that I've been the model Christian who has followed and lived the Word of God to the letter. I wish that I could say that as it stands right now I've done a fantastic job, but I can't. In my situation I've been broken, hurt, angry, bitter, and blinded, I am sure that you can relate. The good news is that today my eyes are open and for that, I can and do give God thanks. Today your eyes are open to being grateful for this moment.

If you want to avoid the pitfalls that I fell into, seek the Lord today and every day. I have allowed my emotions to step in and create spiritual landmines in my life that produced nothing but negativity and toxicity. I'm here to encourage you not to create these same landmines in your life.

When we choose to see God in spite of the negative experiences we face in our life there is always something to be grateful for, we block out the plan of the enemy (which comes to kill, steal, and destroy) in our lives. Every time that we can tell God "thank you," we open ourselves up for healing, restoration, and blessings. We open ourselves up to the miracle that God wants to give us right now.

Think about your situation. What's the truth about it? Write it down. Sometimes just getting it down on paper can help you to release it out of your spirit and present it to God so that He can begin to become Lord over the situation and your life.

_____

_____

_____

_____

_____

_____

_____

_____

_____

_____

_____

_____

_____

_____

_____

_____

_____

_____

_____

_____

Now think about your situation. What can you give God thanks for? I am thankful for an amazing community of sisters that support me daily in prayer and encouragement (my inner circle, if you don't have one I strongly suggest you pray and ask God who they are for you). I'm grateful for my children who love me no matter what situation we are faced with. Most of all I am grateful for a loving, Heavenly Father, who loves me so much and who I can lean on in my times of trouble. I love Him because He first loved me. Are you grateful for some of these same things?

_____

_____

_____

_____

LET US PRAY:

Father in the name of Jesus. Here we are, your children, saying thank you. Thank you for your Son, Jesus, who died that we may have life and have it more abundantly. Thank you, that even when we go through rough patches in our lives, we can look to you to bring us out of them, for you are our deliverer. We ask that you continue to make us whole as we are reminded to give thanks unto you every day of our lives and in every circumstance. We thank you for the understanding that giving you thanks has nothing to do with our emotions, but it has everything to do with our obedience and love unto you. So once again, dear Lord, we thank you for your love; we thank you for your provision, and we thank you for this opportunity to be renewed in our heart, mind, and spirit. In Jesus name, we pray.

AMEN

Do you have a prayer of thanksgiving on your heart today?
Write it down.

_____

_____

_____

_____

_____

_____

_____

_____

_____

_____

_____

_____

_____

_____

_____

_____

_____

_____

Chapter Two

Focused Peace

THE VOICE OF TRUTH:

YOU WILL KEEP HIM IN PERFECT PEACE, WHOSE MIND IS
STAYED ON YOU. BECAUSE HE TRUSTS YOU. (ISAIAH 26:3 NIV)

There are three things that come to my spirit as I read this piece of scripture: (1) We must commit to keeping our mind focused on Jesus. (2) Trust that the Lord will quiet our heart. (3) We must never allow our emotions to be in the driver's seat of our lives. The driver's seat should be reserved for God.

If you're anything like me, you have a lot going on in your life as a woman. Having peace is valuable. I am positive that any time you can get a small pause that is worthy of a deep exhale with closed eyes you can find peace. This very

9

thought is why it is so important for us to learn to live in the abundance of God's peace. When we can live our daily lives in peace, we become better mothers, wives, sisters, employees, bosses, and friends.

Our Lord is so faithful in His love that he teaches us how to have peace every day, every hour, and every minute. WOW! Imagine that. He tells us that if we can commit to keeping our mind on Him, then in return He will not only give us peace, but He will put some extra on it and give us PERFECT PEACE. Thank you, Jesus!

I have learned through my journey with our wonderful Savior that trusting Him has so many benefits. When we focus on God and vow to trust Him, we can be assured that He will take care of whatever issue that we are facing today, tomorrow, and forever. Our hearts become quieted from worry, discouragement, hurt, pain, or any device that the enemy is trying to use to distract us from seeking God and receiving His blessings as we keep our minds on Jesus. We can practice self-control over our emotions.

I heard an awesome woman of God named Priscilla Shier say that "emotions are not intelligent." We definitely should not act on the advice of our emotions. It is by focusing on the Lord through prayer that we should live our lives; this is where our power lies. When we practice this principle, we can't help but win!

I know what you are thinking and trust me, many times I did not have the willpower to stop being emotional and go into prayer. One thing that I love about prayer is that it does not have to be this big event. You don't have to have the choir singing behind you while you go into a 15-minute oration unto God. Sometimes all I can muster out of my mouth is "Jesus Help," and believe me He does just that. I want to encourage you today by letting you know that you will make it. Hold onto the word of God, believe the report of the Lord," that all things work together for the good to them that love God, to them who are the called according to his purpose." (Romans 8:28 NIV)

Sometimes I love to take the Word of God and write it down a few times to commit it to memory so that I can meditate on it when my mind starts to go sideways. (I know I'm not the only one who's mind tries to go sideways!!) What are some ways you can keep your mind on Jesus?

_____

_____

LET US PRAY:

Father God, we love you and thank you for your word today. We thank you for the reminder to keep our mind on you. We thank you that you have assured us that when we practice the principle of keeping our mind on you, that you will reward us with your perfect peace. Lord, help us to always trust in you no matter the circumstance. We pray that you will bring this scripture back to our memory when our mind starts to wander. Write it on our hearts, Lord, and help us to have self-control over our emotions. Let your peace that surpasses all understanding be with us this day and always. In Jesus name, we pray.

AMEN

Do you need more peace in your life? Now is a good time to petition the heart of God. Write your prayer here.

I always find that when I take the time to pray for someone else, the gift of peace is given to me for the labor of love. Do you know someone who could use your prayer for peace in their life? I encourage you to be a blessing today and add them to your prayer.

_____

_____

_____

_____

_____

_____

_____

_____

_____

_____

_____

_____

_____

_____

Chapter Three

Keep Your Head Up!

WORD OF TRUTH:

LIFT UP YOUR HEADS, O YE GATES, AND BE YE LIFTED UP, YE EVERLASTING DOORS, AND THE KING OF GLORY SHALL COME IN (PSALMS 24:7)

This scripture always lifts my spirit when I'm down, disappointed, or discouraged. I guess that is why the Lord put it on my heart to share with you. Do you know that God knows what we are going through and what we need at the precise time that we need it? I am so humbled that He has taken the time to give me such a loving reminder. This scripture encourages me to lift my head and my heart so that Jesus can come in. Right now, I declare it for you and me. In the name of Jesus, BE YE LIFTED UP!!!

15

Sometimes within the blink of the eye, we may need just a little bit of encouragement. We may need a tool to groom the garden of our hearts. I thank God for the day I found this scripture because this word from God has blessed my spirit and I hope that it will bless yours. As you read this passage, allow the words of truth to free you. Use it as a tool to groom any thorns or dead leaves in the garden of your heart. Stop where you are and command your heart, mind, and spirit to be lifted up by Jesus. Let our Lord and Savior consume you with the fullness of His Joy. He's doing it for me. Is He doing it for you? I hope the answer is a resounding yes! If not, maybe you need to acknowledge and receive what is available to you. The joy of the Lord is available to you, which gives us strength. Close your eyes for a few moments. Receive the love and peace that Jesus wants you to have and give thanks for His flow of unconditional love.

We are our own best cheerleaders and encouragers. It is very vital to our physical, mental, emotional, and spiritual well-being to practice being an encourager in our own lives as women of God. Today I challenge you to commit to staying encouraged by the Lord. Command your spirit to be filled with the glory of God and lifted with the spirit of joy throughout your day, week, month, and year. I challenge you to speak the word of truth over yourself every

16

time your flesh wants to get weak. We learn in the word of God that we have the power to speak to those things in our lives that are trying to pull us down. Let every situation know that the joy of the Lord is your strength. Declare the word of God out loud so that the enemy of your soul will know that you are standing on the unbreakable promises of the Almighty God. Right now, declare, "This is the day that the Lord has made. I will rejoice and be glad in it."

What are some other declarations that you can make to encourage yourself today? Write them here, then practice declaring them daily.

_____

_____

_____

_____

_____

_____

_____

_____

_____

_____

_____

_____

_____

_____

_____

_____

_____

_____

LET US PRAY:

Lord God, you are good, and your mercies endure forever. We thank you as we declare your word over our heart, mind, and spirit. We are lifted in you. We declare that every situation in our lives is taken care of in Jesus name. We declare that we will walk in the fullness of your love, joy, and peace. In Jesus name. We declare that we will not allow our emotions to control us, but we will look at our lives through the eyes of your spirit and know that many are the afflictions of the righteous. Heavenly Father deliver us out of them all. We trust you, Lord God. We declare that today we will be encouraged. We will rejoice in you and honor who you are in our lives. In Jesus name, we pray.

AMEN

Treat your spirit today. What prayer of encouragement for yourself is on your heart? Write it here. Meditate on the goodness of God and share it with another woman this week.

_____

_____

_____

_____

_____

_____

_____

_____

_____

_____

_____

_____

_____

_____

_____

Chapter Four

Remember His Unbreakable Love

WORD OF TRUTH:

*NO POWER IN THE SKY ABOVE OR IN THE EARTH BELOW-
INDEED, NOTHING IN ALL CREATION WILL EVER BE ABLE TO
SEPARATE US FROM THE LOVE OF GOD THAT IS REVEALED IN
CHRIST JESUS (ROMANS 8:39 NIV)*

Wow! God is so amazing, and I thank him for his word. What a powerful truth! It is incredible to know that God loves me so much that there's nothing I could do or say to separate him from loving me. When I am feeling weak, unlovable, and alone, my God is faithful and expresses the truth of how He feels about me. When I think about the love that is revealed towards me through Jesus our Lord - my heart sings. Tears fill my eyes to think of how God loves me so faithfully; that He knows me through-and-through. He knows the good, the bad, and the ugly and yet His love never changes. The good news for you today is that He feels the same way about you. Isn't that amazing?

Sister, I'm happy to say that God loves us so much and more than we could think or even imagine. You and I could not begin to wrap our minds around how much love the Father has for us. I'm in awe of this type of the love. The best thing about this revelation is that we can hold onto the promise of His love - especially in times of frustration or times of trouble when our hearts may fail, and we feel all alone. Nothing that we could ever do can separate us from His love.

Today focus in on how God loves you. Worship Him through the truth of this love for you. Know that because of the way that he loves us; it is His will for us to live a life of abundance, free of hurt and pain. He desires for us to live a life free of worry, depression, loneliness, and any other spirit that is unlike Him. These emotions try to weigh us down and block us from having what He says we can have. Freedom.

Are you feeling any of these spirit blockers today? Meditate and ask God to remove anything in your heart that is blocking you from receiving His love and living an abundant life. Write it here.

_____

_____

_____

_____

_____

_____

_____

_____

_____

_____

_____

_____

_____

_____

_____

_____

LET US PRAY

Father in Heaven, we love you because you loved us first. God, we come to you with a heart of repentance for the times we did not recognize your perfect love. We ask your forgiveness for the times we doubted your love for us. We come into agreement with your word of truth that nothing can separate us from your love. As we receive this word, Father we release and forgive ourselves for anything that we have done. Any attitudes we have, we release them now and take on every fruit of the spirit in Jesus name. Father we release hurt, pain, depression, worry, loneliness and every other spirit that does not come from you. We apply the blood of Jesus to our lives, and we declare that this day and forevermore we will walk in the love and abundance given to us by you, our heavenly father. All this we pray in the mighty name of Jesus.

AMEN

Pray about the spirit blockers that the holy spirit revealed to you then receive God's love. Write your prayer here.

_____

_____

_____

_____

_____

_____

_____

_____

_____

_____

_____

_____

_____

_____

_____

_____

_____

_____

_____

_____

Chapter Five

Stand Firm & Win

WORD OF TRUTH:

BUT YOU WILL NOT EVEN NEED TO FIGHT. TAKE YOUR POSITIONS, THEN STAND STILL AND WATCH THE LORD'S VICTORY. HE IS WITH YOU O, PEOPLE OF JUDAH AND JERUSALEM. DO NOT BE AFRAID OR DISCOURAGED. GO OUT AGAINST THEM TOMORROW, FOR THE LORD IS WITH YOU. (2 CHRONICLES 20:17 NIV)

When we are in the middle of struggles, many times it is hard for us to have faith. As I'm going through the battle of finding a job, my money begins to dwindle, and my only mode of transportation breaks down. With four children looking for me to make sure that their needs are met, it would be a natural reaction to go into a panic. And trust me, my flesh reacted and tried to take me there, but thank God for the Holy Spirit that keeps us sane. When we have God on our side, we can lean on His word. His word tells us to stand

27

firm on him; The solid rock. I am reminded that as I stand firm in Him, I don't have to worry about any of the challenges that I am facing. I simply must give them over to Him because He truly does care about me. There is something that you are faced with today so, "go out against it, for He is with you."

Instead of going into panic mode, we can give God praise for the victory over every challenge. As women, more than likely our emotions will want to be in control, but this is our opportunity to show God that we have made Him the head of our lives and that we trust Him to do what he said he would do. Our God is faithful, and I believe that. Do you? We can trust God to place a strategic plan in our spirit to resolve whatever issue may arise. We do not have to fight our own battles because God promised that if we stay in our position and stand still, we will see the Lord's victory manifest in our lives.

I don't know what challenges are confronting you today, but I want you to know that if you stand firm in that increased faith, God will see you through. The good news is that your challenges will disappear, and YOU WILL WIN!

What is our position? Our position is a prayer position. Our position is a faith position. Once we have taken this grand position, our God can and will take it from there. What are you asking the Lord to help you with today? Write it here.

_____

_____

_____

_____

_____

_____

_____

_____

_____

_____

_____

_____

_____

_____

_____

_____

_____

_____

LET US PRAY

Father, in Jesus name we come now with thanksgiving and praise. We come Lord God with love and affection towards you for how you take care of us, your daughters. God, we are thankful that we don't have to fight these battles and trials that arise in our lives. All we have to do is stand still, believe, and see your victory. God, we submit every place of confrontation to you because you said we should not be anxious about anything. Through prayer and supplication with thanksgiving will make our requests known to you. We give it over to you now, and we receive your peace according to the word of truth that says that the Lord will fight for us and hold our peace. Thank you for the peace that surpasses all understanding. Thank you for how you love us. We love you. In Jesus name.

AMEN

What are you in need of today? What are you grateful for? What victory are you expecting in your life? What prayer do you have on your heart?

_____

_____

_____

_____

_____

_____

_____

_____

_____

_____

_____

_____

_____

_____

_____

_____

_____

_____

Chapter Six

Keep Your Mind Right

WORD OF TRUTH:

AND NOW DEAR BROTHER AND SISTERS, ONE FINAL THING.
FIX YOUR THOUGHTS ON WHAT IS TRUE, AND HONORABLE,
AND RIGHT, AND PURE, AND LOVELY, AND ADMIRABLE.
THINK ABOUT THINGS THAT ARE EXCELLENT AND WORTHY OF
PRAISE. (PHILIPPINES 4:8 NIV)

As I'm experiencing a season in the valley, I am learning that keeping my mind in a positive place is vital if I want to make it out on the other side of the storm alive. It is so easy for us to allow ourselves to give in to all of the negative things that we feel in regard to the situations and circumstances that are happening right now, but what I have realized is that God's word comes to give us wisdom and strength. His word will keep us from destruction. The enemy would love to get us distracted with negative things and persuade us to take our eyes off Jesus and the word of God.

In Hebrews 12:2 (NIV) it says, "look unto Jesus, the author, and finisher of our faith." He is the one who wrote the story from beginning to the end, so it would behoove us to make sure that we do what He advises, which is to think positive. I have to tell you, though, that staying positive is not always easy. To be real with you, I have to remind myself sometimes to think of things that are true, right, honorable, and worthy of praise. I command my brain to not think of negative thoughts that my friend Pastor Sheila Dean calls, "stinkin thinkin."

What is helpful and probably critical (especially as a woman) is to have a community of women who can support you, lift you up in the Lord, and empower you to stay positive. Your inner circle is very important. Your inner circles should include people you can trust, and they allow you to be totally transparent without judgment. These are the people who will pray with you and pray for you, and they are the same people who love you when you are up or when you are down (it's what I like to call your "ride-or-dies"). They are 100% loyal and will be with you until the end - no matter what! God always gives everyone someone. Your inner circle is anointed by God to make a positive impact on your life. Again, if you don't know who your inner circle is, I encourage you to pray and ask God to reveal who those people are in your life.

Keeping our minds right during this time will give us the strength to weather the storm. It will help us to be humble and grateful towards God, and it will protect us from becoming bitter, hurt, and angry.

Today I thank God for the reminder to practice positive, holy thinking and for taking my mind off negative thoughts and emotions. I ask Jesus to fix it! After all, He is the one who has loved us before the storm, through the storm, and who will continue in His love for us after the storm has passed. HE IS THE REAL DEAL!! Praise God!

Now say a prayer and ask God to reveal to you the people in your inner circle. Who are those people that are anointed to speak positivity into your life? Write their names here. Ask God how you need to change your thinking. Write what is revealed here.

_____

_____

_____

_____

_____

_____

_____

_____

_____

_____

_____

_____

_____

_____

_____

_____

LET US PRAY

Lord God, thank you for reminding us how important it is to keep our mind in a positive space. We are thankful that you are teaching us how to be intentional in our thinking and how to live out our Christ identity intentionally. Father, we ask that you continue to renew our minds as we practice keeping our minds stayed on you and those things that are pure, honorable, excellent, and true. Continue to help us through those moments when our flesh and emotions would try and steer us in a negative direction. You are the driver of our lives, Lord God. We praise you for your goodness, grace, and mercy. In Jesus name.

AMEN

Chapter Seven

Know He Is Near

WORD OF TRUTH:

THE LORD IS CLOSE TO THE BROKENHEARTED AND SAVES THOSE THAT ARE CRUSHED IN SPIRIT (PSALMS 34:18 NIV)

There is a certain comfort that we get to have as a believer. It is the comfort of knowing that when we are broken-hearted, our Lord is close to us. I thank God today for that closeness and to be able to know that He will save me from the storm.

Beloved, during this time of trouble when the feelings of a broken heart are real to your core, you can rest assure that as we meditate on the word of God and know that He is near, our hearts will begin to feel the soothing power of the anointed oil that God is pouring down on us. I sit with the pain of heartbreak, but there is a quiet comfort in my soul that knows that my God is in control. He has me in His hand.

I hope you can feel the comfort, as well. We can stand on the promise that He saves those that are crushed in spirit. So, if your spirit is crushed, I want to encourage you that this, too, shall pass and that the word of truth is right when it says, "weeping may endure for a night, but joy comes in the morning." The good news is that morning is right now! As you are reading this, God is restoring your heart and giving you joy. Hallelujah!

Friend, we don't have to worry because we can stand on the promise that Jesus came to heal the brokenhearted and to set the captured free (Luke 4:18). We can choose today to live out this truth and be free of the thoughts from negative situations. God is well able to take care of my heart and yours. What is burdening you in your heart today? Tell God all about it. He wants to hear from you. Write it here.

_____

_____

_____

_____

_____

_____

_____

LET US PRAY

Lord, we love you, and we honor you today. We come to you now as your daughters with hearts that have been broken. We come having been let down by people and circumstances. We come having been disappointed, hurt, and sometimes confused as to what is going on in our lives. We turn to you Lord because you are our Father and you care for us. There is no one like you, Lord. No one can make the crooked way straight or mend our hearts, minds, and spirits like you. You hold the King's heart in your hand, so turn our hearts back to wholeness. Heal as only you can in, Jesus name. Help us Lord, so we do not fall into the traps of our negative emotions. We turn everything over to you as we give you thanksgiving and praise. We give you honor and glory in Jesus' mighty name we pray.

AMEN

Do you have a prayer unto God concerning your heart? Write it here and release everything to the Lord.

_____

_____

_____

_____

_____

_____

_____

_____

_____

_____

_____

_____

_____

_____

_____

_____

_____

_____

Chapter Eight

You Are Not A Failure - Get Up

WORD OF TRUTH:

THE GODLY MAY TRIP SEVEN TIMES, BUT THEY WILL GET UP AGAIN (PROVERBS 24:16 NIV)

Sometimes our circumstance can make us feel like a failure-whether it is true or not. Today we can be thankful for the word of truth that God is speaking. Even though we may fail or feel as though we fail, as His children, we will get up again. What an awesome promise! We can mess up as a mother, wife, or friend but God promises that He will give us another chance.

I don't know what battle you are facing right now, but I want to encourage you not to listen to your negative emotions or the whispers of the wicked-one that says you are a failure. You may not have gotten the job done, but our God is faithful to teach us how to obtain the victory. I am learning that each situation that I am put in was ordained. This happens so I can learn how to be the woman of God that I am called to be. Give thanks knowing that God is doing the same thing for you in your life.

Even when we make a mistake and put ourselves in a position that God did not necessarily intend for us to be in, He's faithfully working everything out for our good as we return to obedience towards Him. Because of God's grace and mercy, His loving hand guides us to make the best out of the milk we have spilled, and we overcome every ditch and valley that we find ourselves in. Bless God! Write about a time that you feel you have failed? Then pray and write down how God is leading you to overcome the situation.

_____

_____

_____

_____

_____

_____

_____

LET US PRAY:

Lord, we are overcomers by the blood of the lamb, and we thank you. We pray that every time we begin to have feelings of failure that you will help us to cancel out the thoughts that we are having and replace them with words of truth because we are indeed overcomers. Lord Jesus, you said that in this world we would have tribulations, but we can be of good cheer because you have overcome the world. You have overcome any negativity that tries to invade our lives. You have overcome every mistake we have made and every mistake that we may make in the future. You have overcome even the very situation and obstacle that we are faced with today. Right now, in the name of Jesus we receive your good cheer, we receive your joy, we receive your redemption, we receive your loving kindness, and we receive your blood covering over our lives. We ask that you give us revelation in the lessons we ought to learn out of our circumstances so that we can grow stronger in you and become closer to being just like your son, Jesus. We ask that you help us to learn through this trial and we thank you because we know that we are conquerors like Christ Jesus who strengthens us. We love you, Lord. In Jesus name.

AMEN

Chapter Nine

Trust God

WORD OF TRUTH:

TRUST IN THE LORD WITH ALL YOUR HEART LEAN NOT UNTO YOUR OWN UNDERSTANDING, ACKNOWLEDGE HIM IN ALL YOUR WAYS AND HE WILL DIRECT YOUR PATH. (PROVERBS 3:5-6 NIV)

Many times, when you are going through a trying time, it is easy to lose focus or faith. Well, I'll speak for myself and maybe you can relate. This morning I was reminded to trust in the Lord and not only that, I was reminded that my understanding of the things that I am going through could not be trusted. I need to acknowledge that God, the Father, is Lord of my life and therefore Lord of any battle that comes my way. If I merely hold onto Him, he will lead me to victory.

The same goes for you, my friend. Exercising our faith may not be easy but with everything that we have, we must hold onto the truth that God is faithful and will bring us through many trials and tribulations. Yes, He can bring us out of any negative situation. The key here is to move out of the way and allow God to take us step-by-step to the other side of our situation. Are you unsure in any area of your life? God wants to know about it. Write down your concerns and then accept God as the problem solver that He is.

_____

_____

_____

_____

_____

_____

_____

_____

_____

_____

_____

_____

_____

_____

LET US PRAY

Lord God, we come with gratitude, honor, and praise unto you. We thank you because you know all about what we are going through, and you have not left it up to us to figure things out alone. You have given us the path of peace in the trying times. We acknowledge you in your power, acknowledge you in your sovereignty, and we acknowledge the power of the breakers anointing that flows through you, oh God - the anointing that breaks everything off of us that is unlike you; the anointing that makes everything right. So, we acknowledge you today, Lord God, and we stand now on that promise. We believe that you will reveal to us the solutions and the answers to every concern that we have. Thank you, Father, for the victory over our situation. In Jesus name.

AMEN.

Chapter Ten

Now Faith

WORD OF TRUTH:

NOW FAITH IS THE SUBSTANCE OF THINGS HOPED FOR AND
THE EVIDENCE OF THINGS NOT SEEN (HEBREWS 11:1 NIV)

When I read this scripture this morning, two words jumped out at me. NOW and FAITH. I remember a sermon that I once heard on the very topic. It talked about the importance of having faith right now. Even in the midst of the storm, Now and Faith will propel you forward. As I read the verse, the Holy Spirit brought me back to the first day I realized that I was in the storm. He showed me how far I'd come just by operating in what I like to call - Now-Faith. What is Now-Faith, you may ask? Now-Faith believes in God at this very moment. Now-Faith is not looking at or thinking about minute number two but being present in minute number one and knowing that the hand of God is with you to get you every step of the way. Now-Faith is about trusting God to bring you through. As we meditate on our faith, we can look back at how far the Lord has brought us in our faith. Even though we may be going through something right now, we can rejoice because the word of God says that we serve a God that is the same today as He was yesterday, and forever more. Hallelujah!

Beloved, I want to encourage you today. Believe God like never before for your life and watch Him work it out for your good. It may look dark and gloomy where you are standing, but I can assure you as you continue your journey with the Lord, you will begin to see the clouds in your life disappear and brighter days will be on the horizon. Hold fast to your faith. I once heard Bishop say, "faith is heaven currency," and I have learned that to be true. You may not have the physical resources to get what you need or want in your life right now, but I guarantee that if you just have faith, the mountain can and shall be moved.

Do you believe in what God has especially designed for your life? Are you struggling in your faith? Tell God all about it here.

_____

_____

_____

_____

_____

_____

_____

_____

_____

_____

_____

_____

_____

_____

_____

_____

_____

_____

_____

_____

LET US PRAY:

Dear Heavenly Father, in the name of Jesus, our King, we come humbled and bowed before your throne of grace and mercy. We come saying thank you for being our foundation. We can believe you and do not wish to change you. We pray down, Lord God, for more faith. Not just any faith, Lord God, but Jesus faith. We want to have the same faith that Jesus had as he walked with you here on the earth. We pray for those that are struggling in their faith right now - especially those that are going through a difficult time and trying to hold onto faith to bring them through the fire. God, we pray that you would strengthen them and fortify them, oh God. We bind up the spirit of doubt, and we rest assured that you will perform your word, in Jesus name. Now God, increase our capacity to believe and trust in you. Increase our faith. We love you, Lord and we trust you. We are thankful that your hand is covering every area of our lives. In Jesus name, we pray.

Amen.

Chapter Eleven

Keep Your Eyes On The Lord

WORD OF TRUTH:

OUR GOD, WILL YOU NOT JUDGE THEM? FOR WE HAVE NO POWER TO FACE THIS VAST ARMY THAT IS ATTACKING US. WE DO NOT KNOW WHAT TO DO, BUT OUR EYES ARE ON YOU.
(2 CHRONICLES 20:12b NIV)

Many times when I am faced with trouble, it can feel like a vast army is on my trail ready to attack. Then there are times when one thing after another seems to be coming my way, and I simply don't know what to do. I am sure you can relate.

The awesome thing about being daughters of the Most-High King is that we have a way to escape our troubles by looking to our father in heaven for help. Sister, we don't have to try and solve these issues on our own. All we have to do is keep our eyes on the Lord.

As I write these words to encourage you in your spirit, I am inspired that the ability to keep our eyes on God during times of difficulty is a blessing and part of the journey; it is a blessing not to look at everything that is unfolding in the natural realm. Now, I know keeping our eyes on God is not always easy when all hell is breaking loose in your life. Lord knows that at this time in my life, I have days I want to run away, but it is the keeping power of God that helps me to make it through another day. Loved one, press into that power and lift your eyes to God - the author and finisher of your faith. You can make it and you will. I am standing with you and more than that, you have the greatest intercessor (the Most-High King), interceding on your behalf. Jesus himself is going to the Father and petitioning for him to give you more strength, courage, anointing, grace, power, favor, love, and more of His glory. You have a team of champions behind you, so have no fear. Kick fear to the curb and continue to go forward knowing that as you look to God, "He will fight for you and you shall hold your peace," (Exodus 14:14).

Where in your life do you need to look to God? Write about
it here.

_____

_____

_____

_____

_____

_____

_____

_____

_____

_____

_____

_____

_____

_____

_____

_____

_____

_____

LET US PRAY:

Father in heaven, thank you. We come before you with a heart to repent and to ask you to forgive us for trying to solve these issues without your help and guidance. We ask that you create in us a clean heart and renew us, Lord God. We ask that you would be the head of our lives and that you would help us to keep our eyes on you at this time. Lord, when we feel the need to be the answer, remind us that you alone are the way to the truth and the life. Remind us, Lord God, that we are your children and you are our loving Father. Lord God, we place our lives in your hands, and we are thankful that you have everything under control. We commit today to look toward the hills from which comes our help and we know that the help comes from you. So, we thank you as we give you the praise, honor, and glory that is due to your name. We love you in Jesus name, we pray.

Amen.

Chapter Twelve

How To Go Through The Fire Without Getting Burned

BUT NOW, THIS IS WHAT THE LORD SAYS-HE WHO CREATED YOU, JACOB, HE WHO FORMED YOU, ISRAEL: "DO NOT FEAR, FOR I HAVE REDEEMED YOU; I HAVE SUMMONED YOU BY NAME; YOU ARE MINE. WHEN YOU PASS THROUGH THE WATERS, I WILL BE WITH YOU; AND WHEN YOU PASS THROUGH THE RIVERS, THEY WILL NOT SWEEP OVER YOU. WHEN YOU WALK THROUGH THE FIRE, YOU WILL NOT BE BURNED. (ISAIAH 43:1-2 NIV)

At the beginning of my season of change, I could only see it as a time of hurt, pain, and confusion. I wasn't sure what was going on in my life, but as time went by, I came to understand that it is not just about being hurt, sad, and confused; I think, more importantly, it is a season of transition and transformation. It is about what God wants to

61

do in my life to bring me to that expected end. What you are going through right now is not to destroy you. What you are going through is there to help you develop the character that you need to go to the next level with God.

I now have the revelation and understanding that what I am going through is not just about me going through hard times and feelings of discomfort. I want to share with you what I have learned about getting to the other side of trials without being burned and scarred by the things that happened during the journey. Let me encourage you and say, yes, we can get to the other side without the residue of broken-heartedness, discouragement, and downtroddenness. We can and will come out stronger, better, wiser, and more connected to the spirit of God and our identity in Jesus. I discovered that this is a time of celebration. Yes, I said celebration. How can you celebrate, when you are going through a tough time? Let me explain. The first thing you have to do is....

SURRENDER ALL

I know you are probably thinking, that you have surrendered all in your situation. However, it may seem that your life is currently dark. You may even feel worse than you did when your trials began.

Well, my friend, I was in the same boat. I was going along thinking that I had given everything to God. I felt that I had forgiven everyone and that I had moved on in my life, but suddenly things shattered all around me. The hardest part is that I had no idea that I had not surrendered and allowed God to make me over. I did what I wanted to do, including stuff my feelings down in my soul, and deep in my mind. I had my guard up so I could carry on as if nothing was bothering me. This is the wrong way to handle what is bothering you. If you are doing this, I encourage you to stop right now and cry out to God in the most authentic way you know how.

I have learned that the best thing that you can do when you are going through a challenge is to surrender all to God. As Isaiah 43 verse 2 (NIV) suggests, "give Him everything and let Him have it all." Don't hold anything back whatsoever and lay it all on the line; the good, the bad, and the oh-so-ugly. He wants to hear it all to free us from the weight on our shoulders.

I came to realize that I didn't have to figure it out. I didn't have to always think, "what am I going to do?" because that was not my job and it's not your job either. Once I surrendered everything over to Him, everything changed. God was then able to shape my life and entirely make me over. I would become more like him, in my mind, my heart, and in my spirit.

As a bonus, I came to realize that God loves me so much that he uses my challenges to reveal to me His desire to be intimate with me. Wow! How amazing is that? It is so amazing that I can't even describe it, and that is how our God feels about you, too. He loves you so much that He is revealing to you right now that He wants to be intimate with you; that He wants to take everything that you are carrying and set you free.

Now you know as women, we desire to have intimacy with a man (not just sexual, but intellectual, etc.). Well, the intimacy that you will experience when you allow the Lord to come close will be like no other intimacy that you have experienced before. It is the greatest of all affections that we can have in this life. So, I want to encourage you to pour out your heart and let Him begin the process of transformation.

Journal:

What are you hiding in the depth of your heart? Pour out your heart to God here.

_____

_____

_____

_____

_____

_____

_____

_____

_____

_____

_____

_____

_____

Now that you have poured out your heart to God, I want to share with you something else about surrendering it all. I learned that pouring out my heart to God was only the beginning. We must also realize that we can do nothing to solve the problem. Taking on a position of humility and faith begins the journey to redemption. Let's look at some steps that God has given us to help us navigate through the fire without getting burned.

Let Love Live

Believe it or not, love was and is a significant factor of what has brought me through my time of fire. In a season of my life when everything was so uncertain, my heart was broken, and I didn't know if I was going to be able to pick up the pieces that had shattered. The love of God lifted me up and let me know that I didn't need to pick up the pieces. All I had to do was to trust Him, surrender to Him, and believe that he would ordain my complete healing. I was given hope for the future because of my Fathers consistent, an unwavering certainty of love. He is extending that love to you - even right now. I had no hope in loyalty or trust, but His unconditional love showed me the picture of a loving savior that has never changed. I know now that He will never leave nor forsake me. This taught me that even when people let me down, betrayed me, or have left me to fend for myself - Jesus was standing right there ready for me to take his steady hand so that He could mend every place that I had been hurt.

I want to encourage you that God loves you so much and that no matter where you are in your heart, thoughts, emotions, or in your spirit - He is there with you. The word of God lets us know that He is close to the brokenhearted and saves those who are crushed in spirit. God knows just what to do in our time of trouble, and I am so glad that He does. I can tell you that God is always right on time. He has given me angels to pour into me when I am weak. He has given me angels who come to bless me with their prayers, love, time, talent, and money. When you look around in your life, notice the people that genuinely care about you; the ones who would do almost anything for you. Individuals who really want to see your life blessed. They often hurt when you hurt. Those are your angels. They have been sent by your Heavenly Father to express His love towards you. Do you wonder how they truly understand you? Do you wonder why they can tell you about yourself and you don't get mad? It is because you know that they are only saying it because they love you.

From a women's point of view, no one will hold you down like your sisters in Christ. Now, I know you may have a spouse that is your best friend, but he will never understand you as your sisters do. I am telling you, the team of women that God surrounds you with is amazing. They know how to pray you through, lead when you can't quite see where you are going, and they know how to walk with you when you feel afraid and alone. Their testimonies are there to encourage and inspire you to keep on going. These ladies, or should I say, powerful women of God, know how to hold you down in prayer, faith, love, praise, and worship. These women are authorized to speak power into your life, and they are your inner circle.

As you read this, many of you may be imagining the remarkable women that God has placed in your life and your circle. Bless God right now for those women because I guarantee that you will not be able to get through the fire without them. Cherish them and how they love you. Even in your time of need, be a blessing to them; love on them, and be there for them. Remaining open to who God has placed in my life has helped me stay humble. Humility is definitely one of the tools needed to achieve healing and wholeness in every area of your life.

For those of you who may be reading this and looking around in your life and realizing that you don't share the story of all these amazing women that speak life over you and pray for you - I want you to know they are coming and that I didn't always have that either. The good news is that when I asked God for them, He graciously answered my prayer. You can rest assured knowing that God has someone for everyone. It is possible that you haven't recognized who these women are, or it could be that God is leading you in this season to get connected to a body of believers that can offer you this type of support. Whatever the reason, allow God to show you in prayer how to obtain the desires of your heart. He wants to show you the inner circle of love that he has created just for you; that's how much He cares for you. Remember that the word of God reminds us that God is no respecter of persons. What he does for one, he will do for all. He says whatever you ask in my son's name you shall receive. Isn't it refreshing to know that the Father thoroughly loves us and all we have to do is ask? Yes, He dearly loves us.

There is one more way we can let love live as we journey towards healing and deliverance in our situation, and that is forgiveness. Forgiveness starts with the love of God

69

and is then given to us as it flows through us to the individual or individuals whose actions we deem less than favorable. Consider how God loves us when we stray away, are disobedient, make a mistake or do something unfavorable towards him. Does He hold a grudge, or treat us differently? Of course not! We must heed the example that God has given us and replace the hurt with love. After all, the word of God is right and lets us know that love covers a multitude of sin. The most significant benefit of forgiveness is that we are rewarded with peace and solace in our spirit. When we allow His love to cover those wrongs, we open the door for healing and deliverance to come in. Mostly, we open the door for abundant blessings to flow and we are left with beauty for our ashes. This is a promise from our loving Father.

I encourage you to press into God's love. It is the fundamental launching pad God has for us to get us to the place of complete wholeness.; To bring us through the fires of our lives.

Journal: How can you allow love to live in your life? Who and what do you need to release? Who do you need to forgive?

Put on Faith

My faith in Jesus is the one thing (other than His love for me and my love for Him) that got me through one of the most heartbreaking times of my life. Hebrews 11:1 (NIV), "Now-Faith, for it is the substance of things hoped for and the evidence of things not seen." As long as I had my hope in Jesus, I knew that one day my heart would not ache anymore. One day I would not cry myself to sleep; one day I would be completely whole, and my heart would be healed and restored. I held onto my faith in God, even when my flesh told me that I should not believe. I am here as a living testimony that weeping endures for a night, but joy comes in the morning.

One aspect that I love about faith is how it not only strengthens you as a person - but also your relationship with God.

Now let me be clear that this is true especially when you have a challenge that you are going through. Faith is not easy. It is not easy because while we are spiritual beings, we are flesh. This is why the Bible warns us in the book of Matthew, to watch and pray so that we will not enter into temptation. It says, for the spirit is indeed willing, but the flesh is weak.

If we are not careful during this season, we can quickly get caught up in our flesh (and our emotions) about how we feel about what we are going through. We could solely rely on what we see in the physical realm, instead of keeping our eyes on the truth of what is happening in the spiritual realm. In other words, we must keep our eyes on Jesus, especially in a season where the adversary of our soul wants to make us believe that we are not fighting a fair fight. He wants us to think that we are losing the battle when the truth of the matter is that we have the victory through our Lord and Savior Jesus Christ. He has already won the battle on our behalf as believers in Him. This gives us the confidence to know that we have already won. The Bible tells us that our weapons of warfare are not carnal (they are not of this world, in the physical realm) but are mighty through God to the pulling down of strongholds.

I'm not saying not to be human because that is impossible. What you feel is real, and it is healthy to acknowledge it for what it is, but as believers, we know that emotions are spirits. There is the spirit of anger, the spirit of betrayal, the spirit of grief, the spirit of frustration, and so on - but we have dominion over all of them. We can and must take authority over any spirit that is not like God or His attributes. If we allow negative spirits to rule over us, this will only hinder us from getting to our goal of total and complete healing. And furthermore, we have to understand that these spirits are on assignment to stop us, hold us back, detour us, block us, and destroy us before we reach our full potential in God or reap the benefits that God has promised us. THE DEVIL IS A LIAR!!

That's why I am confident in my faith. It is only by faith that you will be able to overcome all that the enemy has planned for you. It is only by faith in God that you will be able to see your situation from God's point of view and therefore be able to have insight on how to get through it. It is only by faith that you will be able to cast out any spirits that are unlike God.

Yes. Faith is a weapon in your arsenal to fight against the wicked ones. What I love about faith is that it will show Godly insight on how the enemy and his army operate. Because of your faith in God, you will start to see that the more you make an effort to walk towards your healing, the more the enemy will try to bring up your past trials and tribulations. The enemy wants you to hold onto the feelings and emotions that were attached to the incident. Their goal is to get you to hold onto adverse situations to make it impossible for you to manifest healing, restoration, and recovery in your life. This is why the word of God says to submit ourselves to God, resist the devil and he shall flee.

So now, let's talk about how we get faith and how we maintain it. The word of God says that faith comes by hearing the word of God. In this time of challenge, you must find the covering of a church home. You must make it a point to study the word of God. It was hearing the preached word of God and then examining the word for myself that increased my faith and renewed my strength to get through the process of healing. I can truly bear witness to the word of God being the bread of life to feed me and keep me nourished so that I could survive, overcome, and flourish. Once we have faith and that faith has been strengthened, we maintain it by continuing in faithfulness by going to hear the preached word and connecting in the study of the word. Whether that be on our own or in connection with a bible study. Finally, I have learned that incorporating prayer, praise, and worship into my lifestyle has deepened my faith.

These tools that God has provided us has brought me to a place in God that I otherwise would not have tapped into

Journal:

Where are you in your faith? How can your faith be strengthened? What are the steps that you are going to take to test your faith?

_____

_____

_____

_____

_____

_____

_____

_____

_____

_____

_____

_____

_____

_____

_____

_____

Cultivate Prayer Power

Honestly, I could write a whole book on the importance of prayer in a believer's life. Prayer for a person going through the fire is that much more essential, vital, and necessary if you want to get on the other side of your situation with the victory. Prayer is connecting with the Father. It is talking to God and acknowledging that you cannot do it on your own (there's that surrender piece again). It is reverencing His power and ability to change, not only your situation but you as a woman of God. If I could incorporate sound effects in the book (how cool would that be!), I would insert trumpets here.

A strong, powerful prayer life was absolutely my saving grace. And it still is. Developing a prayer life is right up there with having faith. In fact, you cannot establish a prayer life without faith. When you pray, you must believe God by faith and know that He will answer your prayers. Not only is prayer talking to God, but more importantly it is about God talking to us. I can tell you that there were many days and nights where God spoke peace over my heart and mind and reassured me that everything was going to be ok. And more than ok. Even when I saw things in the physical realm that crushed my spirit, it was through prayer and His still, small voice, that the Father spoke his love over me to mend and heal all of the broken places. I want to remind you that our Heavenly Father loves us and desires a relationship with us. That is love is 24-7, 365 days a year. Through the good, the bad, and the ugly - he wants us to talk to him about it all. I have learned through great teaching from my Bishop, Pastor Zachary K. Bruce Sr., that one of the ways to hear God's voice is an ongoing daily conversational relationship with God. Conversation, meaning a two-way form of communication. This is prayer. The bible tells us to pray without ceasing. That is how important prayer is to God, and that is how much he wants to connect with us.

Sometimes, when you are going through something very painful, it is hard to talk to other people about what is going on. But the remarkable thing about prayer is that even when I cannot speak to anyone about my circumstances, there is an open door, through the blood of Jesus, for me to go to God and tell him everything that is on my heart. I am so comforted by that. The thing that I love the most about prayer is that every prayer relationship between God and his children is unique. I don't have to pray like you, and you don't have to pray like me. I can go to God as myself, and

He is well pleased with that. Isn't that something to shout about? Hallelujah!

As I went through my fire, I didn't have the energy to pretend. I am so glad that I don't have to act when it is just God and me. I got down to the nitty-gritty with Him, and he allows me to get it all out. Then he gently strengthens and reassures me. Every time I come out of prayer, even to this very day, I am better. I see what is in front of me in a new way. I am free from the weight that I was holding onto before going to God in prayer. I am changed, I am enriched and equipped to keep going forward. My heart's desire is for you to experience this, too.

At this time, I want to encourage you to develop a consistent prayer relationship with God (if you have not done so already). This book is being published with the hopes that you will use it to either deepen your prayer relationship or start it a new one. I pray that by now you have enjoyed writing your prayers and reflections and that you have begun to love prayer as much as I do.

I am sure that you have noticed that this section of the book is called Cultivate Prayer Power. Cultivating a prayer relationship with God in your life will most definitely bring forth the power of God's anointing. This power is so important because as believers, it is what destroys all of the negative emotions and spirits that we previously discussed. I'm telling you right now, as I was going through pain, it was the anointing of God that kept me sane. It was the anointing of God that allowed me to move to forgiveness; it was the anointing of God that gave me the will to love as Jesus loves; it was the anointing of God that gave me the power to get up out of my bed and have a positive attitude; it was the anointing of God that destroyed every yoke of bondage in my life and brought me to the other side of my brokenness, pain, heartache, discomfort, doubts, and my weakness. It is the anointing of God that can and will do the same for you. The power of God humbles me, and I am in awe of His grace and mercy. He releases His anointing into my life through the power of prayer.

Listen, Sis; I could not possibly say enough about the power of prayer and the importance of having a prayer relationship with God. Not only in times of our trials but really praying without ceasing on a daily basis. Many times, God has moved mountains in my life through prayer. I cannot tell you how many ideas have been birthed through prayer and how many times God has given me a strategic plan to solve the issues in my life through my prayer relationship with Him. Not to mention, the pleasure and sweet intimacy that I experience in the presence of God. It is like no other experience that you will ever have with anyone in this world. It is an experience that will touch you to your very core.

Prayer Power is definitely a must when you're going through the fire. Matter of fact, you will not get through the fire without it.

Journal:

Write about the prayer relationship you have with God. How does it need to grow? What is the spirit of God telling you concerning prayer in your life? What are the action steps you are going to take to cultivate your prayer power?

_____

_____

_____

_____

_____

_____

Get in a Praise Position

Looking up the definition of position in its verb tense I learned that it means to put or arrange (someone or something) in a particular place or way. I'm going to tell you from experience that you are surely going to have to put yourself in a praise position if you expect to come into the complete healing. What I am saying to you is that you have to have the spirit of praise, the mind to praise God, and the heart for praising God. Praising God by faith must become second nature. I know you may be thinking, "How can I do this when I am going through a very hard time in my life?" Be encouraged to know that you can do this. I am reminded that the word of God tells us that we can do all things through our Lord and Savior Jesus Christ. With Faith, you know that it is all working together for your good and you can put your mind on positive things as you give God the glory. Joyce Meyers wrote the book "Battlefield of the Mind." This book is a good starting place if we want to overcome something. Make up in your mind right now that in everything you do, you will give thanks to God.

I started with the small stuff - giving thanks for anything I could find to praise the Lord for.

84

Lord,

Thank you for my hands.

Thank you for waking me up.

Thank you for providing food.

Thank you for my children.

Thank you for my mom.

Whatever you can be thankful for, walk in that until you can finally say "Lord, thank you for this trial that you are allowing me to go through." Simply put, to get in the position of praise we have to believe the word of God about our situation. Once our mind accepts the truth of God's word, we can download it into our heart and hide it there. Now you can access it at any time, as you praise God through the fire.

God not only wants to hear our praise, but praising God is for our good. As we enter into praise, God meets us right there. There is no room for the spirit of heaviness to rest on us. God declares, "for the spirit of heaviness, put on the garment of praise." It is so easy to throw ourselves a pity-party during this time, but rest assured that as we praise

God, we will be refreshed, renewed, and grounded in Christ Jesus. We should be able to sustain a positive attitude, and this is definitely the position we have to maintain to get to the other side. Our mind must be fixed on the goodness of God. It is only when we clear our minds that we can hear and receive instructions from God about the plan he has for us. He will show us how to walk through the valley to the promised land of victory.

Journal:

What are you praising God for today? How can you get yourself in a praise position? How do you feel after your praise God? Reflect on the benefits of praise.

_____

_____

_____

_____

_____

_____

_____

_____

_____

_____

Know who you are

I did not realize this until later in the process, but I want to encourage you. Hopefully, it's early on in your journey through the fire so you can get the benefit that I did not act upon. It's one of those things that you know about instinctively but get lost in the shuffle of life. Honey, you better understand your worth, and you better know who you are. Some situations should not define you and how you feel right now should not define you. If you are a born-again believer, you are a child of God. You are a daughter of the Most-High King. Why does that matter? Because you have kingdom authority and you should use it every day of your life. You have the power to speak to those things that are not what they should be and watch them manifest into what they should be. I'm saying you are unstoppable because you serve an unstoppable God. When they crucified Jesus, they thought that they were stopping the show. But GOD!! Jesus rose on the third day with all of the power in his hands.

No matter what you are going through right now, know that all things are working together for your good. I didn't write that - God did, so please take it to the bank and cash it. Jesus has already paid it all with his blood. Our job is to walk in who He has called us to be with power and with authority. To do that we have to be confident in the one who has given us this power. Romans 8:11(NIV) tells us that, "the same power that rose Jesus from the dead lives inside of us; we can operate in it when we know who we are. "

Journal:

Where have you allowed your power in Jesus Christ to be silenced in your life? What are the action steps that you are going to take to reclaim that power and exercise it in your life?

_____

_____

_____

_____

_____

_____

_____

_____

_____

_____

_____

_____

Let the Journey Continue

I pray that this devotion journal has been a blessing to your life. At this point, I believe that you have a basic toolkit to get through any fire that may ignite in your life - but this is just the beginning. My prayer for you is that you continue to allow God to grow you in faith, love, humility, and prayer. Surrender in every area that would please him. Continue to embrace the beauty of the process that this life has to offer, but always navigate it through Christ Jesus.

I hope that you take these lessons that have been so pivotal in my life and use them to help make changes in yours. Share them with another sister or brother that may need some encouragement along the way on their journey. Share it with those that may not know the Lord but are in need of an escape. I encourage you to continue to journal your prayers and time spent with the Lord. I love going back to old journals and being able to realize the power of God that has brought me a mighty long way.

Sometimes we do get to the other side of our trials before another arises, but it would behoove us to make sure that we are prepared for the next one to come. My bishop teaches us that we are either in a stormy fire, coming out of one, or going into one. The principles in this book are meant to show us how to stay ready. I want to thank you for staying the course, for pushing through, and not giving up. You made it this far, so keep the faith. I am pressing on just like you. Daily. We will always continue to grow as long as we stay on the path to heaven. Be steadfast in that. I love you, and I am always praying for you. Thank you for allowing me to be with you *THROUGH THE FIRE.*

Journal:

Here is one last journal opportunity for you in this book. What was the one take away from this book that changed your life? Who can you bless with that truth? It is a blessing to serve God's people. Always be a blessing to someone.

_____

_____

_____

_____

_____

_____

_____

_____

Made in the USA
Columbia, SC
31 July 2018